ABOUT NORTH CAROLINA...

That magnificent cross section of land of what is best in North America – almost 53,000 square miles in area and about the size of England, the ancestral home of many of its people...
located just south of the State of Virginia and washed by the waters of the Atlantic Ocean of the east, it extends 500 miles to the west with a width of 187 miles at its widest point.
North Carolina, referred to lovingly as the "Tar Heel" State, is divided by nature into three great sections. Along the Atlantic and for a depth of more than 100 miles, it is designated as the coastal region. Here fun from sand and surf lasts from May until mid-autumn.
In the central region, with a depth east and west of about 300 miles, it is referred to as the Piedmont. It is in this section where most of its well kept farms and industries are located.
In the west with a territory about the size of Massachussetts, it is called the Mountain Region or Nature's Wonderland. Here are to be found the Great Smokies and other mountains, capped by Mt. Mitchell rising 6,684 feet, the highest point in Eastern America.
This whole state is blessed with ample rainfall, good soil and an average temperature of almost 60°. Its climate is generally considered unsurpassed for year-round living.
If you were to leave the United States and go overseas with the hope of finding a better place to live than North Carolina, you might find in southern France or northern Italy a similar climate – but you would not find both beauty of landscape and abundance from soil that you find in this fine state.
This longing for Liberty and thanks for Nature's abundance are reflected by the Great Seal of this State, upon which the statue-like figures of Liberty and Plenty stand out in bold relief.
So therefore to all who may visit within its borders –
If you hope to pick a land of ample sufficiency ... a place endowed by Nature's beauty... and a state where its people are taught Liberty and Justice for all –
Visit North Carolina, stay a while and you will want to make this State your home.
by John Locke

Ce splendide "lopin" de terre plus connu sous le nom d'Amérique du Nord... qui s'étend sur une superficie de 53.000 miles carrés, ou presque, soit la superficie de l'Angleterre, demeure ancestrale de nombreux anglais, justement.
Située au sud de la Virginie et baignée par les eaux de l'Océan Atlantique oriental, elle s'étend sur 500 miles à l'ouest et sur 187 miles au point le plus large.
La Caroline du Nord, affectueusement surnommée "Tar Heel State", est naturellement divisée en trois grandes régions. La région côtière d'abord, baignée par l'Atlantique, qui s'étend sur 100 miles dans l'arrière-pays, et où l'on peut venir se détendre et s'amuser sur la plage et sur l'eau à partir du mois de mai et jusqu'au milieu de l'automne.
La région centrale, qui s'étend sur 300 miles environ dans l'arrière-pays, en direction est et ouest, a été baptisée Piedmont. C'est ici que se trouvent les principales fermes et industries de cet état.
La partie occidentale, aussi grande que le Massachussetts, est considérée comme la région des montagnes ou le "pays des merveilles de la nature". C'est ici que s'élèvent le Great Smokies et autres sommets, sur lesquels règne le mont Mitchell qui, du haut de ses 6684 pieds, n'est autre que la plus haute cime de l'Amérique de l'est.
La Caroline bénéficie de pluies abondantes, d'un terrain fertile et d'une température moyenne de 60°F. Son climat est donc agréable tout au long de l'année.
Pour trouver un climat aussi clément, voire encore plus agréable que celui de la Caroline du Nord en dehors des Etats-Unis, il faut aller dans le sud de la France ou dans le nord de l'Italie - sans pour autant retrouver un paysage aussi beau et un terrain aussi fécond que ceux qu'offre cet Etat splendide.
L'"hymne" à la liberté et les dons si généreux que Mère Nature lui a offerts se concrétisent à travers le "Grand Sceau" de cet Etat, sur lequel trônent les statues de la Liberté et de l'Abondance.
Par conséquent, tous ceux qui visiteront cette terre...
Si vous rêvez de grands horizons... d'un site auquel Mère Nature a offert de nombreux "atours"... d'un état dont les habitants croient en la Liberté et la Justice pour tous...
Venez visiter la Caroline du Nord... arrêtez-vous quelques jours et vous sentirez naître en vous le désir d'y bâtir votre demeure.
John Locke

Dieses herrliche Stück Land, das unter dem Namen Nordamerika bekannt ist... mit einer Fläche von fast 53000 Quadratmeilen, die der Großbritanniens gleichkommt, dem Herkunftsland vieler seiner Vorfahren...
Südlich vom Staat Virginia gelegen und vom östlichen Atlantischen Ozean umspült, erstreckt sich sein Gebiet über 500 Meilen nach Westen, bei einer Breite von 187 Meilen an seiner breitesten Stelle.
North Carolina, das liebevoll "Tar Heel State" genannt wird, wird durch die Natur in drei große Regionen unterteilt: die Küstenregion, die sich vom Atlantischen Ozean 100 Meilen ins Landessinnere erstreckt und an deren Ufern das Strand- und Badevergnügen von Mai bis in den späten Herbst dauert.
Die zentrale Region, die sich im Westen und Osten etwa 300 Meilen ins Landesinnere erstreckt, wird Piedmont genannt. Hier haben sichdie meisten Landwirtschafts- und Industriebetriebe dieses Staats angesiedelt.
Der westliche Teil, mit einem Territorium, das der Größe von Massachussetts entspricht, wird Gebirgsregion oder "das herrliche Land der Natur" genannt. Hier liegen die Great Smokies und weitere Gebirgszüge, allen voran der Mount Mitchell, mit seinen 6648 Fuß der höchste Gipfel Ostamerikas.
Im ganzen Staat mangelt es nicht an Regenfällen, der Boden ist fruchtbar und die durchschnittliche Temperatur beträgt 60°F. Sein Klima gilt als ganzjährig ideal.
Wollteman die Vereinigten Staaten verlassen und jenseits des Ozeans nach einem schöneren Ort zum Leben als North Carolina suchen, könnte man ein ähnliches Klima nur im Süden Frankreichs oder in Norditalien finden - nicht aber eine so reizvolle Landschaft und einen solch reichen Boden, wie sie dieser herrliche Staat bietet.
Diese Sehnsucht nach "Freiheit" vereint mit den Gaben einer verschwenderischen Natur sind im "Großen Siegel" dieses Staats dargestellt, bei dem die majestätischen Figuren der Freiheit und des Überflusses im Vordergrund stehen.
Darum gilt für alle, die diesen Staat besuchen...
Wenn Sie eine üppige Landschaft suchen,einen von Naturschönheiten umgegbenen Ort ... einen Staat, in dem die Menschen Freiheit und Gerechtigkeit für alle gelehrt wird...
Besuchen Sie North Carolina ... verweilen Sie eine Zeitlang und Sie werden bald den Wunsch verspüren, für immer hier zu bleiben.
John Locke

北アメリカで最も興味深い造形の妙を見せるこの一角の地域は、古くは多くの先駆原住民の居住地であり、イギリスと等しいほぼ53000 平方マイルの広さを持っている。バージニア州の南に位置し、大西洋の東に裾を濡らし、西に 500マイルの広がりを見せ最も横幅の広い部分は187 マイルに渡る。
ノースカロライナ州は愛着を込めて "Tar Heel State" と呼ばれており、自然により3つの大きな地方に分けられている。海岸地帯は大西洋岸から内陸部に 100マイル入り込み、5月から秋の盛りまで水浴、ビーチを楽しむ事が可能である。
中央部の地区は、東西 300マイルに渡って内陸部に広がる山の裾野の地方である。ここに、この州の大部分の農場や工場が集中している。
マサチューセッツ州とほぼ等しい大きさを持つ西部は、山岳が支配的な自然の楽園でここにグレートスモーキー山岳地帯やアメリカ東部の最高峰、6684フィートを誇るミッチェル山を始めとする他の山々がある。
州全域とも豊富な雨量、肥沃な土壌に恵まれ、気温は平均華氏59度、ほとんど60度であり、年間を通じて温暖であることで有名である。
もし、居住するノースカロライナを後にし、大西洋を渡ってより快適な土地を探すとすれば、よく似た気候を南フランスや北イタリアに見つける事が可能であるが、しかし風光明媚さ、土壌の肥沃さは、この素晴らしい土地の比ではない。
自由への切望、自然の豊穣の地は、自由の像と豊饒の像を象るこの州の印象に象徴されている。
この地を訪問する全ての人に。もし交通網の整備が行き届き、自然美に囲まれ、全ての人々に自由と正義を語る土地がご希望なら、ノースカロライナを訪問することをお勧めする。ここに暫く滞在すれば自ずと、ここをあなたの住いにしたくなる筈である。
John Locke

Aquella esplendida sección de tierra mejor conocida con el nombre de América del Norte ... con una superficie de casi 53000 millas cuadradas, iguales a las de Inglaterra, demora ancestral de mucha de su gente...
Situada al sur del Estado de Virginia y bañada por las aguas del Océano Atlántico oriental, se extiende 500 millas al oeste con una anchura de 187 millas en el punto más amplio.
Carolina del Norte, llamada cariñosamente "Tar Heel State", está dividida, naturalmente, en tres grandes regiones. La costera que desde el Atlántico se extiende por 100 millas hacia el interior; aquí, las diversiones sobre la playa y el agua duran desde Mayo hasta avanzado el Otoño.
La región central, que se extiende por unas 300 millas hacia el interior, hacia este y oeste, viene definida como Piedmont. Aquí están la mayor parte de las granjas y de las industrias de este estado.
La parte occidental, con un territorio de iguales dimensiones que Massachussetts, es denominada la región de las montañas o el "país maravilloso de la naturaleza". Aquí se encuentran las Great Smokies y otras montañas, encabezadas por el monte Mitchell, con sus 6684 pies, la cumbre más alta de América Oriental.
El entero estado goza de abundantes lluvias, de un terreno fértil y de una temperatura media de 60°F. Su clima es normalmente envidiado durante todo el año.
Si se desearan dejar los Estados Unidos e ir al otro lado del océano en busca de un lugar mejor que Carolina del Norte en donde vivir, un clima parecido se podrá encontrar en el sur de Francia o en el norte de Italia - pero no se encontrarán la belleza del paisaje y la riqueza del terreno que este esplendido estado ofrece.
Este anhelo de "libertad" y los dones de una naturaleza generosa están representados en el "Gran Sello" de este Estado, sobre el cual las figuras estatuarias de la Libertad y de la Abundancia resaltan.
Por lo tanto, a todos aquellos que visitarán esta tierra ...
Si deseáis una tierra de grandes medios ... un lugar rodeado por las bellezas de la Naturaleza ... un estado en donde a la gente se le enseña la Libertad y la Justicia para todos ...
Visitad Carolina del Norte ... quedaos un poco y rápidamente aparecerá en vosotros el deseo de hacer de este estado vuestra demora.
John Locke

North Carolina

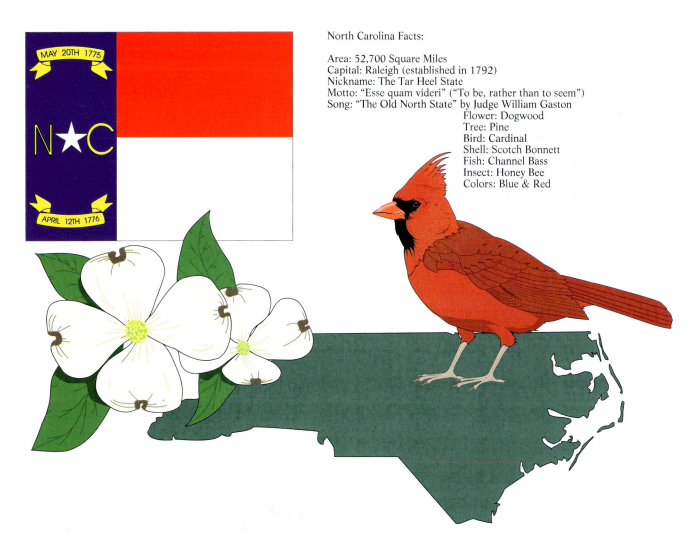

North Carolina Facts:

Area: 52,700 Square Miles
Capital: Raleigh (established in 1792)
Nickname: The Tar Heel State
Motto: "Esse quam videri" ("To be, rather than to seem")
Song: "The Old North State" by Judge William Gaston
Flower: Dogwood
Tree: Pine
Bird: Cardinal
Shell: Scotch Bonnett
Fish: Channel Bass
Insect: Honey Bee
Colors: Blue & Red

Informations sur la Caroline du Nord

Superficie: 52.700 miles carrés
Capitale: Raleigh (fondée en 1792)
Surnom: Tar Heel State
Devise "Esse quam videri" (Etre plutôt que paraître)
Hymne "The Old North State" de Judge William Gaston
Fleur: Sanguinaire
Arbre: Pin
Oiseau: Cardinal rouge
Coquille: Scotch Bonnett
Poisson: Bar
Insecte: Abeille
Couleurs: Bleu et rouge

Daten über North Carolina

Fläche: 52700 Quadratmeilen
Hauptstadt: Raleigh (gegründet 1792)
Spitzname: Tar Heel State
Motto: "Esse quam videri" (mehr sein als scheinen)
Lied: "The Old North State" von Judge William Gaston
Blume: Hartriegel
Baum: Tanne
Vogel: Kardinalvogel
Muschel: Scotch Bonnett
Fisch: Seebarsch
Insekt: Biene
Farben: blau und rot

データで見るノースカロライナ州：

面積： 52700平方マイル
首都：ローリー（1792年建設）
愛称：タール ヒール ステイト
格言： "Esse quam videri" 外観より実質を重んず
歌 ： "ザ・オールド・ノース・ステート" ジャッジ W. ガストン曲
州花：ハナミズキ
州鳥：紅冠鳥
貝 ：スコッチ・ボンネット
魚 ：スズキ
虫 ：蜜蜂
色 ：ブルー＆レッド

Datos sobre Carolina del Norte:

Superficie: 52700 millas cuadradas
Capital: Raleigh (fundada en 1792)
Apodo: Tar Heel State
Lema: "Esse quam videri"(Ser, en vez de parecer)
Canción: "The Old North State" de Judge William Gaston
Flor: Sanguinaria
Arbol: Pino
Pájaro: Cardinal Rojo
Concha: Scotch Bonnett
Pez: Róbalo
Insecto: Abeja
Colores: Azul y rojo

Das Land der farnreichen Wälder, das einst die Mokassins durchstreiften
Das Land der reißenden Flüsse und der fruchtbaren Böden, die reich mit Bauernhöfen besiedelt sind
Das Land, in dem die Unabhängigkeit ein harterkämpftes Recht ist
Das Land, in dem silbrige Gewässer vom Morgengrauen bis zum Sonnen-untergang glänzen
Oh Carolina, geliebtes Land mit sei-nen natürlichen Schönheiten - vom höchsten Berg zum schimmernden Meer - ideales Ziel für Dich und mich.

その昔モカシン族が耕した

シダに覆われる地

農場多く、快活な渓流

草生茂る地

苦難の戦いを経て

独立を勝ち取った地

夜明けから夕刻まで

銀色の水が輝く地

おお、カロライナ、愛する州よ

最も高い峰より光満ちる海まで

玄関先から自然美に溢れる

まさに私に、あなたに相応しい地

The land of fern filled forests where long ago moccasins did trod
The land of sparkling rivers and farm-rich sod
The land where independence is a hard-fought right
The land where silvery waters glimmer from early morn into the night
Oh, North Carolina, the favored state with natural beauty at her gate
– from the tallest mountain to the shiny sea – indeed, it is made for you and me

La terre des forêts truffées de fougères, autrefois foulée par des mo-cassins
La terre des fleuves bouillonnants et des champs herbeux disséminés de fermes
La terre où l'indépendance est un droit acquis à travers de dures ba-tailles
La terre où les eaux argentées brillent de l'aube au coucher de soleil
Oh, Caroline, état élu auquel la nature a prodigué ses dons
- du sommet le plus haut à l'océan lumineux - est faite pour toi et moi

La tierra de los bosques ricos de hele-chos, surcada un tiempo por los mo-casines
La tierra de los rios espumosos y de los campos herbosos ricos de granjas
La tierra en donde la independencia es un derecho adquirido con duras ba-taillas
La tierra en donde las aguas plateadas resplandecen desde el amanecer hasta el ocaso
Oh, Carolina, el predilecto estado con la natural belleza a su puerta
- desde el monte más alto al mar lu-minoso - está hecho propio para mi y para ti.

◄ *Appalachian Trail*
Sentier appalachien
Appalachenweg
アパラチア山脈の小径
Sendero Apalache

From a pristine walk in the Great Smoky Mountains National Park to a trip through the mountain country-side in the fresh greens of spring, or the golden dresses of autumn, you will find the most beautiful trees on earth.
You will find your pleasure; whether it is scenic vistas at Chimney Rock or an exciting ride in the rushing rivers of the Nantahala.

Si vous empruntez le sentier du Parc National des Great Smoky Mountains ou vous traversez les montagnes, vous rencontrerez, parés de la verdure tendre du printemps ou du manteau doré de l'automne, les plus beaux arbres de la terre.Tout ici saura vous réjouir, de la vue panoramique de la Chimney Rock ou de la descente excitante des eaux tumultueuses du fleuve Nantahala.

Auf den Spazierwegen des Nationalparks der Great Smoky Mountains oder beim Wandern durch die Gebirgslandschaft findet man, inmitten von zartem Frühlingsgrün oder eingetaucht in herbstliche Goldtöne, die schönsten Bäume der Welt.
Grund für Freude und Begeisterung gibt es satt. Gleich ob es sich um einen herrlichen Panoramablick vom Chimney Rock oder eine aufregende Fahrt durch die wilden Wasser des Nantahala Flusses handelt.

グレートスモーキー山岳国立公園の小径を歩いたり、山間の村を通過して、春の清々しい緑や、秋の黄金のベールの中に浸ると、そこここに地上で最も美しい木々が見られる。
チムニー・ロックのパノラマや、刺激的なナンタハラ川の、奔流下りなど楽しみは尽きない。

Recorriendo un sendero originario en el Parque Nacional de las Great Smoky Mountains o atravesando el paisaje montañoso, sumergidos en el verde tierno de la primavera o en el manto dorado del otoño, encontraréis los árboles más bellos de la tierra.
Encontraréis siempre un motivo de júbilo, sea que se trate de una vista panorámica de la Chimney Rock o de un descenso emocionante en las aguas tumultuosas del rio Nantahala.

▼ *Lake Junaluska*
Junaluska See
Lac Junaluska
ジュナラスカ湖
Lago Junaluska

▼ *White Water Rafting*
Rafting sur le White Water
Rafting auf dem White Water
ホワイト・ウォーターでのいかだ下り
Rafting sobre el White Water

Chimney Rock Park overlooking Lake Lure
Le Parc de Chimney Rock surplombe le lac Lure
Der Chimney Rock Park überragt den Lure See
ルール湖の上に広がるチムニー・ロック公園
El parque de Chimney Rock domina el Lago Lure

▼ *Maggie Valley*
マッジー　ヴァァリー

▲ Maggie Valley is a delight to all throughout the year. Friendly people, mountain crafts and good food are just a few of the offered treats that may be found on a visit.

Maggie Valley est un véritable délice en toute saison: habitants accueillants, artisanat local, excellente gastronomie, voilà ce qui vous attend, entre autres, si vous décidez de visiter la région.

Maggie Valley ist das ganze Jahr über ein echtes Vergnügen: freundliche Leute, lokales Kunstgewerbe, ausgezeichnetes Essen sind nur einige der zahllosen Attraktionen dieser Region.

マッジー　ヴァリーは一年中どの季節でも素晴らしい。感じ良い人々、地の工芸職人、美味しい料理などはこの地方を訪問する人が得られる楽しみのほんの一例である。

Maggie Valley es delicioso en cualquier época del año: gente amistosa, artesanía local y óptima comida, son algunos de los deleites que se os ofrecerán si visitáis esta región.

Great Smoky Mountains

▼ *Rhododendron*
シャクナゲ

▶ *Split Rail Fence*
Clôture à joints métalliques
Zaun mit Metallverbindungen
金属製の接続部のある囲い
Recinto con juntas de metal

Just as a butterfly emerges from a chrysalis, so do the Great Smoky Mountains change from a stark white blanket into an explosive spring. Four distinctly beautiful seasons await exploration. Rugged barns, historic cabins, snow dusted split-rail fences of days gone by, cool mists of waterfalls and breath-taking flora are all part of nature's finest show piece in the Great Smoky Mountains National Park.

Wie eine Larve sich zum Schmetterling wandelt, so mutieren die Great Smoky Mountains von der starren weißen Schneedecke zu einer überwältigenden Explosion von Frühlingsfarben. Vier Jahreszeiten, jede mit ihrem eigenen Reiz, wollen bewundert werden. Heuscheunen, historische Hütten, alte, schneeüberstäubte Zäune mit Metallverbindungen, von Wasserfällen aufsteigende Nebelschwaden und eine atemberaubende Flora sind Teil des prachtvollen Naturschauspiels, das der Nationalpark der Great Smoky Mountains bietet.

Tout comme un papillon qui s'échappe de sa chrysalide, les Great Smoky Mountains abandonnent leur blanc manteau au profit d'une formidable explosion de couleurs printanières. Ici, les quatre saisons sont toutes aussi admirables. Des granges, des maisons historiques, d'anciennes clôtures dont les joints métalliques sont encore saupoudrés de neige, des cascades bouillonnantes et une flore à couper le souffle, voici quelques uns des atouts que Mère Nature a offert au Parc National des Great Smoky Mountains.

まさにサナギから生まれる蝶のように、グレートスモーキー山岳地帯も純白の硬い覆いから素晴らしい春の色彩の氾濫へと脱皮する。四季それぞれの美しさが訪問者を待つ。干し草庫、歴史的な小屋、雪を払除けた金属製の接続部のある囲い。滝から立上ぼる霧、息をのむ花の数々は、グレートスモーキー山岳国立公園の自然の輝かしいショーの一こまである。

◀
Indian Creek near Deep Creek
Indian Creek non loin de Deep Creek
Indian Creek in der Nähe von Deep Creek
ディープ・クリークにあるインディアン・クリーク
Indian Creek en los alrededores de Deep Creek

▶
Ravencliff Falls
Cascades Ravencliff
Die Ravencliff Wasserfälle
ラヴェンクリフの滝
Cascadas Ravencliff

Como una mariposa emerge de la crisálida, así las Great Smoky Mountains mutan de un pesado manto blanco a una formidable explosión de colores primaverales. Cuatro estaciones, con la propia belleza individual, esperan para ser admiradas. Graneros, cobertizos históricos, viejos recintos con juntas de metal espolvoreados de nieve, nieblas que se alzan desde las cascadas y una flora que quita el aliento, forman parte de una de las más esplendidas exhibiciones de la naturaleza en el Parque Nacional de las Great Smoky Mountains.

Mingo Falls near Cherokee ▲
Cascades Mingo non loin de Cherokee
Die Mingo Wasserfälle in der Nähe von Cherokee
チェロキーにてミンゴの滝
Cascadas Mingo en los alrededores de Cherokee

▼ *Oconaluftee Visitors Center*
Centre visiteurs Oconaluftee
Besucher-Center Oconaluftee
オコナラフティー・ビジターズセンター
Centro visitantes Oconaluftee

▲ *Fontana Lake*
Lac Fontana
Fontana See
フォンターナ湖
Lago Fuente

The Blue Ridge Parkway

The Blue Ridge Parkway is truly one of nature's most wonderful gifts to mankind in that a wild, natural plant and animal kingdom is only slightly interrupted by an expertly designed winding highway, which traverses from Virginia to North Carolina through some of the most beautiful scenery in the world.

One may encounter drifting fog one moment and then a rainbow the next. Large, out-croppings of rocks are around every bend. Vistas beg you to stop your car and take a breath of cool, crisp air as your eyes are dazzled by the endless landscape. Blue mist envelopes the rolling peaks and valleys and no greater treasure awaits you than the setting sun melting into pinks, crimsons and golden candle light. You wish time would freeze the view for you, but even so, you can take a mental picture and hold the memory until it is erased by yet an even more spectacular sunset.

La Blue Ridge Parkway est vraiment un des dons les plus magnifiques que la nature a fait à l'homme, un royaume encore vierge de plantes et d'animaux, effleuré par une route intelligemment conçue qui, de la Virginie, traverse la Caroline du Nord et permet d'admirer un des paysages les plus pittoresques du monde.

Ici, un banc de brume peut immédiatement être suivi d'un arc-en-ciel. Dans chaque virage, on rencontre un amas de pierres. Le panorama est si beau que le visiteur est contraint de descendre de voiture et de respirer un grand bol d'air frais tout en se laissant subjuguer par l'immensité du paysage. Une brume bleu enveloppe les cimes ondulées et les vallées et rien n'est plus beau qu'un coucher de soleil où se mêlent les roses, les tons cramoisis et la lumière dorée. On voudrait que le temps s'arrête, mais il suffit peut-être de photographier mentalement cette merveille pour en garder un souvenir émerveillé, jusqu'à l'arrivée d'un nouveau coucher de soleil.

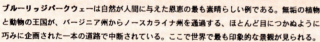

ブルーリッジパークウェーは自然が人間に与えた恩恵の最も素晴らしい例である。無垢の植物と動物の王国が、バージニア州からノースカライナ州を通過する、ほとんど目につかぬように巧みに企画された一本の道路で中断されている。ここで世界で最も印象的な景観が見られる。

濃い霧の後に虹が見られる事がある。各々の曲り角には岩の塊がある。パノラマは、訪問者に車を停止させ、新鮮なぴちぴちとした空気を思う存分吸い込ませずにはおかない。広大な景観に目が眩む。うねる山頂と谷をブルーの微かな霧が覆い、ローズ色、深紅に黄金の光をまぶしながら沈む入り日ほど荘厳で貴重な瞬間はない。おそらく時間が停止して、そのイメージを残して欲しいと願われることだろう。だがこのように瞬時であっても別のスペクタクルな入り日の光景がとって替わるまでは瞼に焼きつけ、記憶に残すことは可能である。

La Blue Ridge Parkway es verdaderamente uno de los dones más espléndidos que la naturaleza haya hecho al hombre, un reino incontaminado de plantas y animales, interrumpido de forma casi imperceptible por una carretera proyectada inteligentemente, que desde Virginia atraviesa Carolina del Norte en uno de los paisajes más sugestivos del mundo.

Se puede encontrar un banco de niebla y al poco, ver un arco iris. En cada curva hay montones de rocas. El panorama obliga al visitante a parar el coche y a tomar un poco de aire fresco y puro, mientras los ojos se deslumbran por la inmensidad del paisaje. Una neblina azul rodea las cimas onduladas y los valles y no existe tesoro más grande a esperaros, que el sol que tramonta mezclándose al rosa, carmesí y a la luz dorada. Desearéis que el tiempo conserve esa imagen para vosotros, pero podéis fotografiarla mentalmente y conservarla en el recuerdo hasta que otro espectacular ocaso vaya a sustituirla.

Die Blue Ridge Parkway ist wirklich eines der schönsten Geschenke, das die Natur dem Menschen hinterlassen hat, ein unberührtes Reich von Pflanzen und Tieren, durch das kaum sichtbar eine perfekt in die Natur integrierte Straße führt, die North Carolina inmitten einer der schönsten Landschaften der Welt durchquert.

Man kann durch eine Nebelwand fahren und sofort danach einen Regenbogen sehen. Hinter jeder Kurve harren Felsenmassen. Das prachtvolle Panorama zwingt den Besucher anzuhalten und tief die frische, prickelnde Luft einzuatmen, während seine Augen von der überwältigenden Landschaft geblendet werden. Ein feiner, bläulicher Dunst verhüllt die welligen Gipfel und Täler und es gibt nichts Grandioseres als die untergehende Sonne, die sich hier in unvergeßlichen Rosa- und Rottönen mit dem goldenen Abendschein vermischt. Man wünscht, die Zeit möge dieses Bild auf ewig aufbewahren, man möchte es im Geist photographieren und aufheben, bis ein nächster, spekatulärer Sonnenuntergang es verblassen läßt.

▼ *Mt. Pisgah Panorama*
Vue du mont Pisgah
Ausblick von Mount Pisgah
ピスガ山のパノラマ
Vista del monte Pisgah

▲ Hornbuckle Tunnel
Galerie d'Hornbuckle
Hornbuckle Galerie
ホルンバックルのトンネル
Tunel de Hornbuckle

▼ Autumn Splendor
Splendeur automnale
Herbstliche Pracht
華麗な秋
Esplendor otoñal

The Blue Ridge Parkway

A rising mountain mist encompasses the Blue Ridge Parkway to provide a picturesque view on every turn.

Après dissipation de la brume qui enveloppe la Blue Rigde Parkway, on peut admirer un beau panorama après chaque virage.

Der Nebel, der den Blue Ridge Parkway einhüllt, lichtet sich und gibt hinter jeder Kurve den Blick frei auf ein herrliches Panorama.

ブルーリッジパークウェーを包む霧が晴れて、曲り角ごとにパノラマを望むことができる。

La niebla que cubre la Blue Ridge Parkway se aclara y permite admirar un bello panorama en cada curva.

► Mt. Mitchell is the highest mountain in eastern America and stands 6,684 feet.

Du haut de ses 6.684 pieds, le mont Mitchell domine toute la côte Est des Etats-Unis.

Der Mount Mitchell ist mit seinen 6684 Fuß der höchste Gipfel Ostamerikas.

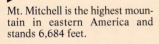

ミッチェル山は東部アメリカ最高峰で、6684フィートある。

El Monte Mitchell es la cima más alta de América Oriental con sus 6684 pies.

Mt. Mitchell
Mont Mitchell
Mount Mitchell
ミッチェル山
Monte Mitchell

The Upper Falls, Yellowstone Prong at Graveyard Fields are captured in a spectacular array of autumn splendor.

Les Upper Falls, Yellowstone Prong, dans les Graveyard Fields, immortalisées dans une exibition suggestive de splendeur automnale.

Die Upper Falls, Yellowstone Prong in den Graveyard Fields in einer prachtvollen Herbstaufnahme.

グレーブヤードにて。優美な秋の印象的なショーの中で不朽にされたアッパーの滝とイエローストーンの支流

Las Upper Falls, Yellowstone Prong, en Graveyard Fields, inmortalizadas en una sugestiva exhibición de esplendor otoñal.

▲*Table Rock*
テーブル　ロック

▶

Winter Blue Ridge Parkway
La Blue Ridge Parkway en hiver
Winterliche Ansicht des Blue Ridge Parkway
ブルーリッジパークウェーの冬の情景
Vista invernal de la Blue Ridge Parkway

The Blue Ridge Parkway

◄ *Grandfather Mountain with Linn Cove Viaduct*
Le Mont Grandfather et le viaduc Linn Cove
Mount Grandfather mit dem Viadukt Linn Cove
グランドファーザー山とリン・コーブの桟橋
Monte Grandfather con el viaducto Linn Cove

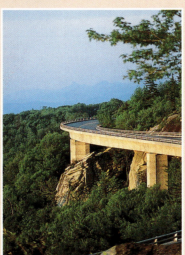

The Linn Cove Viaduct (right) is one of the world's engineering marvels. It is truly a great masterpiece of the Blue Ridge Parkway, and blends in beautifully with nature.
The Linville Gorge is one of the few areas in the country designated by Congress as a wilderness area and prohibits encroachment of any kind by man. The sheer cliffs are among the steepest in the country, and autumn is one of the best times of the year to visit.

Le viaduc Linn Cove (à droite) est une des merveilles du génie civil. Il s'agit d'une véritable oeuvre d'art de la Blue Ridge Parkway, qui se fond avec la nature en parfaite harmonie.
La Gorge Linville est un des rares sites protégés, sur ordre du Congrès américain, où l'homme n'a absolument pas le droit d'intervenir. Les escarpements verticaux, ou presque, sont pratiquement les plus abrupts des Etats-Unis. L'automne est une des meilleures saisons pour visiter cette région.

Das Viadukt Linn Cove (rechts) ist einer der prächtigsten Ingenieurbauten der Welt, ein wahres Kunstwerk des Blue Ridge Parkways, das sich harmonisch in die Natur einfügt.
Die Linville Schlucht ist einer der seltenen Orte des Landes, die vom Kongress zum Naturschutzgebiet erklärt wurden und in dem jeder menschliche Eingriff verboten ist. Die fast waagerecht abfallenden Hänge gehören zu den steilsten des Landes. Ein Besuch dieses reizvollen Gebiets lohnt sich besonders im Herbst.

リン・コーブ陸橋（右）は世界の建造物の中でも驚嘆に値する一つであり、自然のハーモニーに溶込むブルーリッジパークウェーの正真正銘の芸術品である。
リンビルの峡谷は、議会が一切の人工的介入を禁止している、国内でも数少ない特別保護地域である。ほとんど真っ逆様の断崖は国内で最も険しい岩崖の一つで、秋はこの地区の訪問には最適の季節の一つである。

El viaducto Linn Cove (a la derecha) es una de las maravillas de la ingeniería civil del mundo. Se trata de una verdadera obra de arte de la Blue Ridge Parkway, que se mezcla armoniosamente con la naturaleza.
La Garganta Linville es una de las pocas localidades del país designada por el Congreso como área protegida, en donde al hombre se le ha prohibido cualquier tipo de intervención. Los despeñaderos casi verticales son los más escarpados del país. El otoño es una de las épocas mejores para visitar esta zona.

High Country

Explore Blowing Rock and learn the legend. Take in an incredible vista at Cone Memorial along the Blue Ridge Parkway. Enjoy fabulous mountain shopping and excellent dining in Boone and Blowing Rock Village, as well.

Visitez Blowing Rock et découvrez la légende. Profitez de la vue incroyable qui s'offre à vous du Cone Memorial, le long de la Blue Ridge Parkway. Laissez vous tenter par l'artisanat local et un excellent repas à Boone et Blowing Rock.

Besuchen Sie Blowing Rock und lassen Sie sich seine Legende erzählen. Genießen Sie die herrliche Aussicht vom am Blue Ridge Parkway liegenden Cone Memorial. Lassen Sie sich von den reizvollen typischen Kunstgewerbeartikeln und dem ausgezeichneten Lunch in den Dörfern Boone und Blowing Rock in Versuchung führen.

Cone Memorial ▲ コーン・メモリアル

ブローイング・ロックを訪問しこれに纏わる話を聞こう。ブルーリッジパークウェー沿いにあるコーンメモリアルからの信じ難いパノラマを満喫しよう。土地の職人の手仕事による製品や、ブーン村、ブローイング・ロック村での、申し分のない食事を楽しもう。

Visitad Blowing Rock y aprended la leyenda. Asimilad la increible vista que se goza desde Cone Memorial, a lo largo de la Blue Ridge Parkway. Gozad de los fabulosos artículos de artesanía local y de la excelente comida en la calidad de Boone y Blowing Rock.

Blowing Rock ▼
ブローイング・ロック

▲ *Boone*
ブーン

▼ *Chetola Lake*
Lac Chetola
Der Chetola See
チェトラ湖
Lago Chetola

Pilot Mountain
Mont Pilot
Mount Pilot
パイロット山
Monte Pilot

Tobacco Barn
Magasin de tabac
Ein Tabaklager
タバコの納屋
Almacén de tabaco

North Carolina is blessed with wonderful state parks. Pilot Mountain is a large monadnock, that rises 1,500 feet above the surrounding area, and is located near Mount Airy, famous for "Andy of Mayberry."
Hanging Rock State park offers panoramic views, sparkling mountain streams, waterfalls, cascades and of course, rock climbing.

La Caroline du Nord est truffée de splendides parcs nationaux. Le mont Pilot est un grand monadnock qui s'élève à 1500 pieds, non loin du mont Airy, qu'"Andy of Mayberry" a rendu célèbre.
Le Parc National Hanging Rock vous offre des vues panoramiques, des torrents de montagne bouillonnants, des cascades et, bien entendu, la possibilité de faire de l'escalade.

North Carolina ist reich an herrlichen staatlichen Parks. Der Mount Pilot ist ein großer Monadnock, der 1500 m über das umliegende Gebiet ragt und in der Nähe des Mount Airy liegt, der durch "Andy of Mayberry" berühmt wurde.
Der staatliche Park Hanging Rock bietet Panorama-Ausblicke, schäumende Gebirgsbäche, Wasserfälle und selbstverständlich optimale Climbing-Gelegenheiten.

Hanging Rock State Park
Parc gouvernemental d'Hanging Rock
Der staatliche Hanging Rock Park
ハンギングロック州立公園
Parque estatal de Hanging Rock

ノースカライナ州には州立の多くの美しい公園がある。パイロット山は大きな残丘で "Andy of Mayberry" で有名なエアリー山の近くにあり、周囲の地から1500フィート上に聳えている。

Carolina del Norte es rica de esplédidos parques estatales. El monte Pilot es un grande monadnock que se eleva 1500 pies sobre la zona que lo rodea y se encuentra cerca del monte Airy, famoso por "Andy of Mayberry".
El Parque Estatal Hanging Rock ofrece vistas panorámicas, torrentes espumosos de montaña, cascadas y, naturalmente, la posibilidad de hacer climbing.

The Biltmore Estate

One of our national treasures, the Biltmore House, is located in Asheville, and visitors can enjoy this glorious mansion throughout the four seasons from the spring tulip explosion to the Christmas lights, decorations, and holiday activities.

Biltmore House, véritable trésor national, se trouve à Asheville. Les visiteurs pourront apprécier la beauté de cette glorieuse demeure tout au long de l'année: de l'explosion des tulipes au printemps aux décorations lumineuses de fin d'année.

Einer unserer Nationalschätze, Biltmore House, liegt in Asheville. Besucher können dieses prachtvolle Anwesen das ganze Jahr besichtigen: vom Tulpenmeer im Frühjahr bis zum festlichen Weichnachtsschmuck.

国宝の一つビルトモア・ハウスはアッシュビルにある。訪問者は春のチューリップの氾濫光と飾りに包まれるクリスマス、休日の活動に至るまで年間を通じてこの栄光の住居を観賞できる。

Uno de nuestros tesoros nacionales, la Biltmore House, se encuentra en Asheville. Los visitantes podrán admirar esta gloriosa demora durante todo el año: desde la explosión de tulipanes en primavera, a las luces y adornos de navidad, hasta las actividades festivas.

Asheville Land of the Sky

These are the misty hills and cool mountain streams that have inspired Carl Sandburg and Thomas Wolfe whose homes are open to the public.

Ces collines brumeuses et ces torrents glacés de montagne ont inspiré Carl Sandburg et Thomas Wolfe, dont les maisons sont ouvertes au public.

Die nebligen Hügel und kalten Gebirgsflüsse, die Carl Sandberg und Thomas Wolfe inspirierten, deren Wohnsitze besichtigt werden können.

霧の濃い丘と山の冷たい奔流が、カール・サンドバーグやトーマス・ウォルフを刺激した。彼等の家は一般に公開されている。

Las colinas neblinosas y los frios torrentes de montaña que han inspirado a Carl Sandburg y a Thomas Wolfe, cuyas residencias están abiertas al público.

Carl Sandburg Home
カール・サンドバーグの家

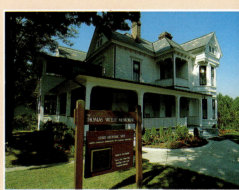

Thomas Wolfe Memorial
トーマス・ウォルフ・記念館

One of North Carolina's greatest treasures are her abundant wildlife and beautiful horses - both domestic and wild. Our state bird is the firey cardinal, and our national and state parks provide safe and natural homes to many wild animals that have been part of our country for hundreds of years. (Fishing is among the finest in the nation with everything from fresh water trout found in our rushing streams to surf fishing for blues on the Outer Banks.)

Un des principaux trésors de la Caroline du Nord n'est autre que la nature sauvage et ses splendides chevaux - élevés en liberté. Notre oiseau fétiche est le cardinal rouge et nos parcs nationaux offrent un abri sûr et naturel aux nombreux animaux sauvages qui peuplent ce territoire depuis des centaines d'années. (Cet Etat est un véritable paradis pour les pêcheurs, de la truite qui frétille dans les eaux douces et turbulentes des torrents au brochet des Outer Banks).

Zu den größten Schätzen das Staates gehören seine üppige, wilde Natur und seine rassigen Pferde, die teils gezüchtet werden, teils in Freiheit aufwachsen. Unser Vogel ist der Kardinalvogel und unsere National- und staatlichen Parks bieten zahllosen Wildtieren, die seit Jahrhunderten unser Land bevölkern, ein sicheres, naturbelassenes Habitat. (Der Fischfang gehört hier zu den reichsten des ganzen Landes, von der Süßwasserforelle der reißenden Gebirgsbäche zu den Hechten der Outer Banks).

ノースカロライナの主要な富には原生の豊富な自然と、素晴らしい馬、（飼育された馬とほとんど野生に近い馬の両方）がある。州鳥は紅冠鳥で、我々の国立、州立公園は何百年も前から国の一部を形成している多くの野生の動物に自然で安全な住家を提供している。（奔流の流れ、軟水に棲む鱒からアウター・バンクスでのカワカマス釣まで、魚はおそらく国内で一番豊富である。）

Uno de los principales tesoros de Carolina del Norte está formado por la rica naturaleza salvaje y por sus esplendidos caballos - criados en estado bravo. Nuestro pájaro es el cardenal rojo y nuestros parques nacionales y estatales ofrecen una demora segura y natural a los numerosos animales salvajes que forman parte de nuestro país desde hace cientos de años. (La pesca es quizás la más abundante de toda la nación; desde la trucha que vive en las aguas dulces y turbulentas de los torrentes, a la pesca del lucio sobre las Outer Banks).

Charlotte, The Queen City
Charlotte - La ville de la reine
Charlotte - Die Stadt der Königin
シャーロット –女王の町
Charlotte - La ciudad de la reina

Discovery Place
発見された場所

Charlotte is truly the "Emerald City" in the wonderland of American Cities and is the largest city in the two Carolinas.

Au pays des merveilles des villes américaines, Charlotte est vraiment la "ville d'émeraude" et la plus grande métropole des deux Caroline.

Charlotte ist wirklich die "Smaragd-Stadt" der amerikanischen Städte und auch die größte Stadt der beiden Staaten North und South Carolina.

シャーロットは真にアメリカの魔法の国の中の"エメラルドの町"であり、二つのカロライナ州の中で最大の都市である。

Charlotte es realmente la "ciudad de esmeralda" en el país encantado de las ciudades americanas y es la ciudad más grande de las dos Carolinas.

Charlotte Coliseum ▲
Colisée Charlotte
Das Charlotte Colosseum
シャーロットの円形競技場
Coliseo Charlotte

Omnimax Theater ▶
Théâtre Omnimax
Das Omnimax Theater
オムニマックス劇場
Teatro Omnimax

Charlotte Motor Speedway ▲
Voie rapide Charlotte
Autobahn von Charlotte
シャーロットの自動車競技場
Autovía Charlotte

Charlotte, Queen City

Not only is the City historically founded and named for Queen Charlotte, but also is the home of NBA basketball and NFL football. Cheer on your favorite race car driver at the Charlotte Motor Speedway, tour historic Fourth Ward, or enjoy exciting water sports on one of Charlotte's three fresh water lakes (Norman, Wylie and Mountain Island) that surround the city.

Cette ville, qui porte le nom de la Reine Charlotte, possède également une équipe de basket NBA et une équipe de football NFL. Venez admirer votre pilote de course préféré sur le Charlotte Motor Speedway, visiter le Fourth Ward ou pratiquer un des nombreux sports nautiques excitants sur un des trois lacs (Norman, Wylie et Mountain Island) qui encerclent la ville.

Die Stadt ist nicht nur historischen Ursprungs und trägt den Namen der Königin Charlotte, sondern ist auch Sitz der Basket Ball Mannschaft NBA und der Fußballmannschaft NFL. Begeistern Sie sich für Ihren Lieblingsfahrer bei den Autorennen am Charlotte Motor Speedway, besuchen Sie den historischen Fourth Ward oder treiben Sie Wassersport an einem der drei Seen von Charlotte (Norman, Wylie und Mountain Island), die rund um die Stadt liegen.

歴史的な起源やシャーロット女王の名ばかりではなく町はバスケットボールのチームNBAやフットボールチームNFLのホームでもある。シャーロットのレーシングカー競技場でひいきのパイロットの技を楽しもう。歴史的なフォース・ワードの訪問も良いしシャーロットの周囲を囲む3つの湖（ノーマン、ウィリー湖、マウンテン・アイリンド）の一つでスリル満点な水のスポーツを楽しもう。

No sólo la ciudad posee un origen histórico y lleva el nombre de la Reina Charlotte, sino que también es la residencia del equipo de baloncesto NBA y del de fútbol NFL. Gozad de vuestro piloto preferido de coches de carreras sobre el Charlotte Motor Speedway, visitad el histórico Fourth Ward o practicad los excitantes deportes acuáticos en uno de los tres lagos de Charlotte (Norman, Lago Wylie y Mountain Island) que rodean la ciudad.

Hezekiah Alexander Home
La maison d'Hezekiah Alexander
Das Haus von Hezekiah Alexander
ヘゼキア　アレキサンダーの家
Casa de Hezekiah Alexander

Winston Salem

Winston-Salem is a delightful city, rich in culture and history.
Wake Forest, a nationally renown university, is located here as well as many other highly accredited colleges.

Winston-Salem est une ville délicieuse, empreinte de culture et de traditions.
Elle accueille la Wake Forest, une université réputée à l'échelle nationale, ainsi qu'un grand nombre d'autres collèges tout aussi célèbres.

Winston-Salem ist eine reizvolle, kultur- und geschichtsträchtige Stadt.
Hier liegen Wake Forest, eine auf nationaler Ebene anerkannte Universität, und zahlreiche andere, ebenfalls renommierte Colleges.

ウィンストン －サレムは文化と歴史の色濃いとても優美な町である。ここにウェイク・フォーレスト、国内でよく知られた大学があり、他にも同様に有名なカレッジが数多くある。

Winston - Salem es una ciudad deliciosa, rica de cultura y de historia.
Aquí se encuentra la Wake Forest, universidad reconocida a nivel internacional, así como otros muchos colleges igualmente reconocidos.

Reynolda House
Maison Raynolda
Reynolds House
レイノルダの家
Casa Reynolda

Old Salem

Old Salem is an 18th Century Moravian Congregational town. Founded in 1766, it is a historic treasure of quaint buildings. Through painstaking restoration, Old Salem has been preserved for visitors to actually experience the feeling of how it may have been to live in the town over two hundred years ago.

Old Salem est une des villes de la Congrégation de Moravie du XVIIIe siècle. Fondée en 1766, c'est un écrin historique pour de nombreux édifices pittoresques. Grâce à une savante restauration, Old Salem a retrouvé tout son charme de façon que les visiteurs puissent plonger dans le quotidien de leurs ancêtres qui vivaient ici il y a deux cent ans.

Old Salem ist eine Stadt der Mährischen Brüder aus dem XVIII. Jahrhundert. 1776 gegründet, stellt sie einen historischen Schatz an pittoresken, liebevoll restaurierten Gebäuden dar, die den Besucher mitten in das Leben von vor 200 Jahren zurückversetzten.

オールドサレムは18世紀のモラビア派信徒の集会に起源を持つ町である。町は1766年に建設され、情感溢れる家のある歴史記念物である。細心の修復作業を経てオールドサレムは訪問者が200 年以上も前の生活を彷彿とすることができるように保存されている。

Old Salem es una ciudad de la Congregación de Moravia del siglo XVIII. Fundada en 1766, es un tesoro histórico de edificios pintorescos. Gracias a una minuciosa tarea de restauración, Old Salem ha sido conservada para que los visitantes puedan revivir la experiencia de una forma de vida de hace doscientos años.

Salem Square with School ▲
La Place de Salem et l'école
Der Salem Platz mit Schule
サレム広場と学校
Plaza Salem con la escuela

Winkler Bakery ▲
Boulangerie Winkler
Die Bäckerei Winkler
ウィンクラーのパン屋
Panadería Winkler

North Carolina Zoological Park

A new world. The North Carolina Zoo has been described by experts as "the zoo of the next century," and a model for future zoos.
Our exhibits let you experience the wonder and excitement of wildlife from both Africa and North America.

Un nouveau monde. Les experts en la matière ont baptisé le zoo de la Caroline du Nord "le zoo du XXIe siècle". C'est un exemple pour les zoos du futur.
Ici, vous pourrez admirer les merveilles et vous plonger dans l'univers sauvage de l'Afrique et de l'Amérique du Nord.

Eine neue Welt. Der Zoo von North Carolina wird von Experten als "Zoo des XXI. Jahrhunderts" beschrieben und stellt ein richtungweisendes Modell für alle künftigen Tiergärten dar.
In diesem Ambiente bekommt man einen lebensnahen Eindruck von den Abenteuern der Wildnis in Afrika und Nordamerika.

新しき世界。ノースカロライナの動物園は専門家から〝21世紀の動物園〟と称され、未来の動物園のモデルを成している。この環境の中で北アメリカとアフリカの自然を愛で、興奮する野生生活体験を得ることが可能である。

Un mundo nuevo. El zoo de Carolina del Norte ha sido descrito por los expertos como "el zoo del siglo XXI" y constituye un modelo para los zoos del futuro.
En este ambiente se podrán admirar maravillas y vivir la excitación de la vida salvaje de Africa y América del Norte.

The city of High Point is the hosiery and furniture capital of the world, as well as the home of the North Carolina Shakespeare Festival where one can experience local, national, and international productions.

La ville d'High Point, capitale mondiale de l'industrie des meubles et de la maille, accueille le Festival Shakespearien de la Caroline du Nord qui met en scène des productions locales, nationales et internationales.

Die Stadt High Point, weltweit berühmt für ihre Möbel- und Strickwarenindustrie, veranstaltet das Shakespeare Festival, das lokale, nationale und internationale Inszenierungen aufführt.

ハイポイント市は家具とメリヤス織の世界的産地であり、ノースカロライナ州のシェークスピア・フェスティバルがあり、地元の作品や国内、外国の芝居を観賞することができる。

En la ciudad de High Point, capital mundial de la industria de muebles y de géneros de punto, se celebra el Festival Shakesperiano de Carolina del Norte que pone en escena producciones locales, nacionales e internacionales.

Fayetteville, N.C. is a delightful city - famous for the Old Market House and Museum of Art erected in 1838. Also, nearby is Fort Bragg, a U.S. Army Base.

Fayetteville, N.C., est une ville gracieuse réputée pour sa Old Market House et son Musée d'Art construit en 1838. Non loin de là se dresse Fort Bragg, une base de l'armée américaine.

Fayetteville, N.C. ist ein reizvolles Städtchen, das für sein Old Market House und das 1838 erbaute Kunstmuseum berühmt ist. Ganz in der Nähe liegt Ford Bragg, eine amerikanische Militärbasis.

フェイエットビルN．C．はオールド・マーケット・ハウスと1838年に建設された美術館で有名な可愛い町である。近くにはフォーグ・ブラッグ、合衆国軍基地がある。

Fayetteville N. C., es una graciosa ciudad famosa por el Old Market House y por el Museo de Arte, edificado en 1838. En las cercanías, Forg Bragg, una base del ejercito de los Estados Unidos.

Greensboro is the site of the Guilford Courthouse National Military Park where one of the most decisive battles of Revolutionary War took place. The Greensboro Historical Museum features extensive displays of war relics, pioneer items, and Indian relics, as well as O. Henry and Dolley Madison exhibits.

Greensboro accueille le Parc Militaire National Guildfort Courthouse, où eut lieu une des batailles décisives de la Guerre d'Indépendance des Etats-Unis. Au Musée Historique de Greensboro, on peut admirer des reliques de guerre, des objets ayant appartenu aux pionniers ou aux indiens, ainsi que des expositions de O. Henry et Dolley Madison.

Greensboro beherbergt den Nationalen Militärpark Guilford Courthouse, wo eine der entscheidenden Schlachten des Amerikanischen Unabhängigkeitskriegs stattfand. Das Historische Museum von Greensboro stellt Erinnerungsstücke an den Krieg, die Zeit der Pioniere und Indianer und Werke von O. Henry und Dolley Madison aus.

グリーンズボロにはギルドフォード・コートハウス国立軍事公園がある。ここで、アメリカ独立戦争の決定的な戦いが繰広げられた。グリーンズボロ歴史博物館には、戦争の遺物、開拓者の遺品、インディアンの遺品などが展示され O．ヘンリー、ドリー・マディソンの展示もある。

En Greensboro se encuentra el Parque Militar Nacional guildford Courthhouse en donde tuvo lugar una de las batallas decisivas de la Guerra de la Independencia Americana. El Museo Histórico de Greensboro expone reliquias de guerra, objetos de los pioneros, reliquias indias y acoge las exposiciones de O. Henry y Dolley Madison.

Goldsboro, incorporated in 1847, was named for Major Matthew T. Goldsborough, civil engineer for the Wilmington and Weldon Railroad. It is also the home of Seymour Johnson Air Force Base.

Goldsboro, dotée de statuts en 1847, doit son nom au Major Matthew T. Goldsborough, ingénieur civil du chemin de fer Wilmington et Weldon. Elle accueille notamment la base aéronautique Seymour Johnson.

Goldsboro, deren Statut auf das Jahr 1847 zurückgeht, wurde nach Major Matthew T. Goldsborough benannt, dem Bauingenieur der Eisenbahn von Wilmington und Weldon. Hier liegt auch der Luftstützpunkt Seymour Johnson.

ゴールズボロは1847年に創設されたが、ウィルミントンやウェルダンの鉄道を施設した技師メジャー・マチューT．ゴールズボローの名に因んでいる。シーモア・ジョンソン空軍基地がある。

Goldsboro, dotada de estatuto en 1847, toma el nombre del Mayor Matthew T. Goldsborough, ingeniero civil del ferrocarril Wilmington y Weldon. En donde se encuentra también la base aeronáutica Seymour Johnson.

Raleigh, the Capital City

Raleigh is located in the heartland of North Carolina. Not only is it the state capital, but it is the home of the North Carolina Museum of Arts and North Carolina State University.

Raleigh, la capitale, se situe en plein cœur de la Caroline du Nord. Elle accueille notamment le Musée des Arts de la Caroline du Nord et l'Université d'Etat de la Caroline du Nord.

Raleigh, im Herzen von North Carolina, ist die Hauptstadt des Staats. Hier befinden sich auch das Kunstmuseum North Carolinas und die Staatliche Universität von North Carolina.

ローリーはノースカロライナの中心にある。州都であるばかりでなく、ノースカロライナ芸術館や、ノースカロライナ州立大学の所在地でもある。

Raleigh, en el corazón de Carolina del Norte, es la capital del estado. Acoge también el museo de las Artes de Carolina del Norte y es la sede de la Universidad Estatal de Carolina del Norte.

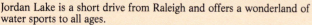

Jordan Lake is a short drive from Raleigh and offers a wonderland of water sports to all ages.

Non loin de Raleigh, Jordan Lake offre la possibilité de pratiquer des sports nautiques à tout âge.

Jordan Lake, in der Nähe von Raleigh, ist ideal für sämtliche Wassersportarten.

ローリーの近くにあるジョーダン湖、全ての年齢に相応しい水のスポーツを楽しめる。

Jordan Lake, en los alrededores de Raleigh, ofrece la posibilidad de practicar deportes acuáticos para todas las edades.

Duke University Hospital ▲
Duke University Hospital
Das Duke University Hospital
デューク大学病院
Duke University Hospital

Universities

Duke University is located in Durham, NC. One of the leading colleges of higher education in the world, Duke University leads the way with research and technological advances in the medical field. The campus is beautifully designed and it is renown for its gothic Duke Chapel with a carillon of 50 bells in the 210 ft. tower.

La Duke University, à Durham, NC, est un des collèges les plus importants du monde. Elle est en effet leader en matière de recherche et de progrès technologique dans le domaine médical. Le campus, magnifiquement aménagé, est réputé pour la Duke Chapel gothique et son carillon de 50 cloches situé dans une tour de 210 pieds de haut.

Duke University in Durham N.C. ist eines der berühmtesten Colleges der Welt. Die Duke University ist auf dem Gebiet der technologisch-medizinischen Forschung absolut führend. Das großzügig angelegte Campus ist bekannt für die gotische Duke Chapel, mit ihrem Glockenspiel aus 50 Glöckchen im 210 Fuß hohen Turm.

デューク大学はダーラムNCにあり、世界で最も重要な大学の一つである。特に医学分野での技術研究開発では世界のリーダー格である。美しい設計のキャンパスは50鐘のカリヨンのある210フィートの塔を備えるゴシック様式のデューク教会で有名である。

Duke University en Durham N.C. es uno de los más importantes college del mundo. Duke University es lider en investigación y progreso tecnológico en el campo médico. El campus, espléndidamente proyectado, es famoso por la gótica Duke Chapel con un carillon de 50 campanillas en la torre, alta 210 pies.

▲*The Dean Smith Center - University of North Carolina - Chapel Hill*
Le centre Dean Smith à l'Université de la North Caroline - Chapel Hill
Das Dean Smith Centre an der Universität von North Carolina - Chapel Hill

ディーン・スミス・センター、ノースカロライナ大学 チャペルの丘

El centro Dean Smith en la Universidad de North Carolina - Chapel Hill

Duke Chapel
Chapelle Duke
Die Duke Kapelle
デューク教会
Capilla Duke▼

NC State University　ＮＣ州立大学

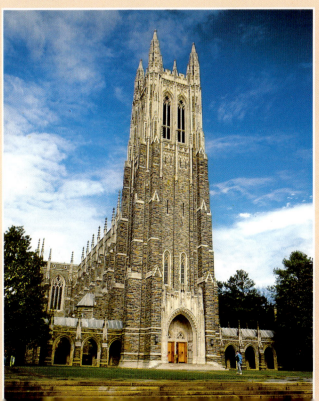

The season of spring in North Carolina is hard to match anywhere else. From the cool greenery of the North Carolina mountains throughout the Piedmont and into the coastal towns of Wilmington and New Bern, spring dogwood, cherry blossoms and azaleas abound. The "showy" flowers compete for one's attention and provide a great feast for the eyes.

Der Frühling in North Carolina ist unvergleichlich. Vom frischen Grün der Gebirgsketten durch das Piedmont bis zu den Küstenstädten Wilmington und New Bern sind die prachtvollen Blüten von Hartriegel, Kirsche und Azalee ein wahrer Augenschmaus.

ノースカロライナの春は比類がない。山の新鮮な緑から、山の裾野を通抜け ウィルミントンやニューバーンの海浜の町まで花ミズキ、桜、アザレヤが咲 き乱れる。花のショーは目を楽しませてくれる祭りである。

La primavera en Carolina del Norte no tiene igual. Desde el fresco verde de las montañas de Carolina del Norte a través del Piedmont hasta las ciudades costeras de Wilmington y New Bern, sanguinarias, flores de cerezos y azaleas, abundan. Las pomposas flores son una fiesta para la vista.

En Caroline du Nord, le printemps est plus beau qu'ailleurs. De la verte fraîcheur des montagnes du Piedmont, jusqu'au villes côtières de Wilmington et New Bern, les sanguinaires, les fleurs de cerisier et les azalées sont reines et offrent un spectacle enchanteur.

Spring explodes into summer colors and wild flowers. A mountain favorite is the spectacular rhododendron. A drive along the Blue Ridge Parkway would provide any visitor an enjoyable view of rhododendron, mountain laurel, dogwoods, azaleas and much more, depending on the season.

A la fin du printemps, les couleurs et les fleurs de l'été explosent littéralement. Le rhododendron en est un exemple fantastique. Une promenade en voiture le long de la Blue Ridge Parkway vous permettra d'admirer des rhododendrons, des lauriers, des sanguinaires, des azalées et autres fleurs, selon la saison.

Der Frühling bricht aus mit sommerlichen Farben und Blüten. Eine der schönsten ist der prachtvolle Rhodendron. Bei einer Autofahrt über den Blue Ridge Parkway kann man die herrlichen Rohodendronbüsche, die Lorrbeerbäume, Hartriegel, Azaleen und je nach Jahreszeit zahllose andere blühende Pflanzen bewundern.

春は、突然夏の花と色彩に成代わる。山の愛される花の一つにシャクナゲがある。ブルーリッジパークウェーをドライブすれば、シャクナゲ、月桂樹、花ミズキ、アザレヤその他多くの花を季節によって楽しむことができる。

La primavera hace explosión en los colores y en las flores del verano. Uno de los favoritos es el fabuloso rododendro. Una excursión en coche por la Blue Ridge Parkway permitirá admirar rododendros, laureles, sanguinarias, azaleas y muchas otras flores, según la estación.

Fabulous Plantations and Gardens

Tryon Palace at New Bern, NC was North Carolina's first official capital and royal governor's residence. Termed "the most beautiful building in either of the Americas" in its day, Tryon Palace has been restored with period furnishings and perfectly manicured gardens.

Le Tryon Palace à New Bern, NC, a été la première résidence officielle du gouverneur de la Caroline du Nord. Décrit à l'époque comme la "plus belle demeure d'Amérique", Tryon Palace a été restauré, meublé dans un style d'époque et ses jardins magnifiques sont parfaitement entretenus.

Tyron Palace in New Bern, N.C. war der erste offizielle Wohnsitz des Gouverneurs von North Carolina. Damals als "das schönste Gebäude Amerikas" beschrieben, wurde Tyron Palace restauriert und stilgerecht möbliert. Sein gepflegter Park ist sehenswert.

ニューバーンのトリオン・パレス。ＮＣはノースカロライナ州総督の最初の公式の官邸が置かれた。当時、"アメリカで最も美しい館" と書かれたトリオンパレスは、修復され、当時の家具と手入れの行き届いた庭園を持つ。

El Tryon Palace en New Bern. N.C. ha sido la primera residencia oficial del gobernador de Carolina del Norte. Descrito en su época como "el palacio más bello de América", Tryon Palace ha sido restaurado con muebles de la época y jardines perfectamente cuidados.

▲ *Orton Gardens*
Jardin Orton
Die Orton Gärten
オルトン庭園
Jardines Orton

▼ *Elizabethan Gardens*
Jardins élisabéthains
Elisabethanische Gärten
エリザベシアン庭園
Jardines isabelinos

The world famous Elizabethan Gardens are located along the Outer Banks at Manteo. The gardens were created and are maintained by the Garden Club of North Carolina, Inc., and are a memorial to the Elizabethan men and women sent by Sir Walter Raleigh to colonize the new world.

Les célébres Jardins Elisabéthains se trouvent à Manteo, dans l'Outer Banks. Projetés et entretenus par le Garden Club of North Carolina Inc., ils sont dédiés aux hommes et aux femmes élisabéthains envoyés par Sir Walter Raleigh pour coloniser le nouveau monde.

Die berühmten Elizabethan Gardens liegen in Manteo, Outer Banks. Der Park wurde vom Garden Club of North Carolina Inc. angelegt und wird auch heute noch von ihm gepflegt. Er ist den elisabethanischen Männern und Frauen gewidmet, die Sir Walter Raleigh ausgeschickt hatte, die neue Welt zu besiedeln.

エリザベシアン庭園はアウターバンクスのマンテオにある。庭園はノースカロライナガーデンクラブにより設計され手入れされている。新世界植民地化のためサー・ワルター・ローリーによって送られて来たエリザベス時代の男女を記念している。

Los famosos Elizabethan Gardens se encuentran en Manteo, en Outer Banks. Los jardines han sido proyectados y son cuidados por el Garden Club of North Carolina Inc. y están dedicados a los hombres y mujeres isabelinos enviados por Sir Walter Raleigh para colonizar el nuevo mundo.

Airlie Gardens ▼

Orton Plantation ▶

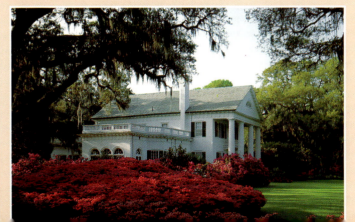

Pinehurst

Amidst the majestic pines and the profusion of blooming azaleas, Pinehurst beckons the world class golfer or amateur alike to participate in a round of golf.

Au milieu des pins majestueux et d'une profusion d'azalées en fleur, Pinehurst invite les amateurs à participer à un tournoi de golf.

Unter den majestätischen Pinien und inmitten einer Fülle von blühenden Azaleen, lädt Pinehurst Golfliebhaber zu einem Golfturnier ein.

厳めしい松や咲乱れるアザレヤの間でパインハルストは、世界的なゴルファーやゴルフ愛好者をトーナメントに誘う。

Entre los majestuosos pinos y la abundancia de azaleas en flor, Pinchurst invita a los amantes del glof a participar a un torneo de glof.

Beaufort, North Carolina is the third oldest town in North Carolina. Much of the flavor and charm of an 18th century seacoast town has been retained in Beaufort for the visitor to enjoy.

Beaufort est la troisième ville antique de la Caroline du Nord. La beauté et le charme de cette ville côtière du XVIIIe siècle ont parfaitement été perpétués, pour la plus grande joie des visiteurs.

Beaufort, N.C., ist die drittälteste Stadt von North Carolina. Pracht und Charme der Küstenstadt aus dem XVIII. Jahrhundert sind zur Freude der Besucher erhalten geblieben.

ノースカロライナのボーフォートは州 3 番目の歴史の古さを誇る。輝かしい18世紀の海浜の町はその魅力を保存し訪問者を喜ばせる。

Beaufort, Carolina del Norte, ha sido la tercera ciudad antigua de Carolina del Norte. El esplendor y el lujo de la ciudad costera del siglo XVIII ha sido conservado para el gozo del visitante.

eautiful coastal towns dot early the entire 300 miles of oastline between Virginia and outh Carolina.

es 300 miles de côte qui 'étendent entre la Virginie et la aroline du Sud sont criblés de plendides petites villes.

eizvolle Küstenstädtchen lie-en an dem 300 Meilen langen üstenstreifen zwischen Virgi-ia und South Carolina.

ージニア州とサウスカロライナ州の間 300マイルの海岸に美しい町々が並ぶ

splendidas ciudades costeras urgen en las 300 millas de cos- entre Virginia y Carolina del ur.

Elizabeth City is a historic coastal town with beautiful sights and delicious seafood.

Elizabeth City est une ville côtière historique aux panoramas splendides et aux délicieux poissons.

Elizabeth City ist eine historische Küstenstadt, berühmt für ihr Panorama und ihren Fisch.

エリザベスシティーは歴史的な海の町で、素晴らしいパノラマと美味しい魚が魅力である。

Elizabeth City, es una histórica ciudad de la costa con espléndidos panoramas y pescado exquisito.

Wilmington is located along the Cape Fear River, and is a fast growing international port city. Also, known for the historic homes district, Wilmington is a "must see" during the spring azalea festival!

Wilmington, en bordure de la Cape Fear River, est un port international en plein essor, réputé, entre autre, pour ses maisons d'époque. Il faut absolument venir le visiter pendant le festival du printemps des azalées.

Wilmington liegt am Cape Fear River und ist ein sich rasch entwickelnder internationaler Hafen. Bekannt auch für seine schönen alten Wohnhäuser, sollte man Wilmington unbedingt im Frühjahr zur Azaleenblüte besuchen.

ウィルミントンはケープ・フィア川に沿ってあり、ダイナミックに拡大中の世界的な港である。
歴史的建造物でも有名なこの町の訪問はアザレヤ祭のある春を欠かす事ができない。

Wilmington surge a lo largo del Cape Fear River y es un puerto internacional en rápida expansión. Conocida también por sus residencias de época, no se puede no visitar Wilmington durante el festival de primavera de las azaleas.

UNC-Wilmington   *UNC -ウィルミントン*

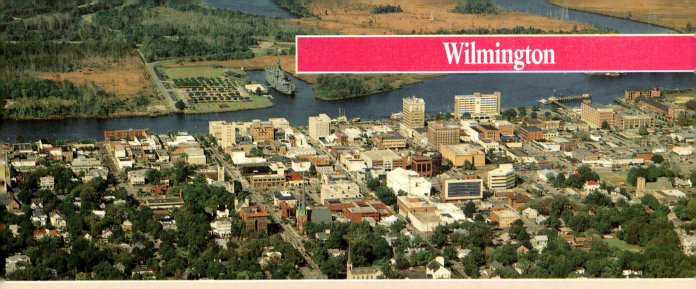

Wilmington

The Battleship USS North Carolina

When the keel of NORTH CAROLINA was laid in October of 1937, she was the first battleship to be constructed in sixteen years. She became the first of ten "fast battleships" to join the fleet in Wolrd War II. NORTH CAROLINA and her sister ship, WASHINGTON, comprised the NORTH CAROLINA Class. At the time of her commissioning on 9 April 1941, she was considered the world's greatest sea weapon. Armed with nine 16 inch guns in three turrets and twenty 5 inch 38 caliber guns in ten twin mounts, NORTH CAROLINA proved a formidable weapons platform. Her wartime complement consisted of 144 commissioned officers and 2,195 enlisted men, including about 100 Marines.

Quand le navire NORTH CAROLINA fut lancé en 1937, c'était le premier navire de guerre construit en seize ans. Il devint le premier des "dix bateaux de guerre" qui rejoignirent la flotte pendant la Seconde Guerre mondiale. NORTH CAROLINA et son jumeau WASHINGTON constituent la NORTH CA-ROLINA Class. Le 9 avril 1941, date à laquelle il fut armé, il était considéré comme le plus grand bateau de guerre du monde. Equipé de 9 mitrailleuses de 16 pouces installées dans trois tourelles et de 20 mitrailleuses calibre 38 dans dix supports couplés, NORTH CAROLINA était une formidable plate-forme armée. En temps de guerre, son équipage était constitué de 144 officiers et de 2.195 soldats, dont 100 Marines.

Als das Schiff NORTH CAROLINA 1937 vom Stapel gelassen wurde, war es das erste Kriegsschiff, das in sechzehn Jahren gebaut wurde. Es war das erste von "zehn Kriegsschiffen", das im zweiten Weltkrieg die Flotte erreichte. Die NORTH CAROLINA und ihr Zwilling WASHINGTON stellen die NORTH CAROLINA Class dar. Am 9. April 1941, dem Datum, an dem es mit Waffen ausgerüstet wurde, galt es als größtes Kriegsschiff der Welt. Ausgerüstet mit 9 16-Zoll, in drei Türmen installierten Maschinengewehren und 20 Maschinengewehren des 38er Kalibers war die NORTH CAROLINA eine phantastische, bewaffnete Plattform. Ihre Besatzung bestand zu Kriegszeiten aus 144 Offizieren und 2.195 Einberufenen, darunter 100 Marines.

ノースカロライナ号が1937年に進水された当時は16年間で造船された始めての戦艦であった。第二次世界大戦の艦隊を成す10隻の戦艦の第一番目の戦艦であるノースカロライナ号とその姉妹艦ワシントン号はノースカロライナ等級を成す。1941年4月9日戦闘用意指令を受けた当時は世界最大の戦艦であった。3つの塔に9台の16インチ砲と、10の砲射台に対に20の5インチ38口径砲を装備していた。ノースカロライナ号は素晴らしい武装基艦であり、乗組員は戦争当時 144人の士官と 100人の海兵隊員を含む2195人の召集兵を数えた。

Cuando el buque NORTH CAROLINA fue botado en 1937, era el primer buque de guerra construido en dieciséis años. Fue el primero de "diez buques de guerra" a alcanzar la flota en la Segunda Guerra Mundial. NORTH CAROLINA y el gemelo WASHINGTON, constituyen la NORTH CAROLINA Class. El 9 de Abril de 1941, fecha en la cual fue armado, era considerado como el más grande buque de guerra del mundo. Equipado con 9 ametralladoras de 16 pulgadas instaladas en tres torretas y 20 ametralladoras calibre 38 en diez soportes acoplados. NORTH CAROLINA era una formidable plataforma armada. Su tripulación en tiempos de guerra estaba formada por 144 oficiales y 2.195 enrolados, de entre los cuales 100 Marines.

Outer Banks

Dominating Cape Hatteras National Seashore (right), the Cape Hatteras Lighthouse is open to the public. This 193 foot brick tower built in 1870 affords a sweeping panoramic view of the "Graveyard of the Atlantic."

Hatteras is one of the more popular fishing villages along the East Coast and a stopping off place to Ocracoke Island by ferry.

Standing majestically on Kill Devil Hill in the distance, the 60' monument honors the Wright Brothers flight of the first powered airplane, Dec. 17, 1903. After assembly in the nearby buildings, this historic first flight remained aloft 12 seconds and flew a total distance of 120 feet.

Aircraft has advanced amazingly since the first successful powered flight. Here at the museum near the Wright Brothers' National Memorial, visitors can relive that first dramatic flight as they see the authentic replica of the Wright Brothers Airplane.

Le Phare du Cap Hatteras, qui domine le Cape Hatteras National Seashore, est ouvert au public. Cette tour en briques de 193 pieds de haut construite en 1870 offre une vue splendide sur le "Cimetière de l'Atlantique". Hatteras est un des villages de pêcheurs les plus célèbres de la Côte Est, où il faut impérativement s'arrêter avant d'aller sur l'île Ocracocke.

Majestueusement érigé sur la Kill Devil Hill, le monument de 60' célèbre le vol effectué par les Frères Wright sur le premier aéroplane à moteur, le 17 décembre 1903. Construit dans des hangars situés non loin de là, il resta en vol pendant 12 secondes sur une distance totale de 120 pieds.

Depuis, l'aviation a fait beaucoup de progrès. Dans le musée situé près du Monument National des Frères Wright, les visiteurs pourront revivre ce premier vol à travers la reproduction de l'aéroplane de ces pionniers de l'aviation.

Der die Cape Hatteras National Seashore (rechts) überagende Leuchtturm von Cape Hatteras kann besichtigt werden. Dieser 193 Fuß hohe und 1870 erbaute Backsteinturm blickt über den "Friedhof des Atlantiks".

Hatteras ist eins der berühmtesten Fischerdörfer der Ostküste und beliebte Etappe auf dem Weg zur Insel Ocracoke.

Sich majestätisch über dem Kill Devil Hill erhebend, feiert das 60' hohe Denkmal den Flug der Gebrüder Wright vom 17. Dezember 1903 im ersten Motorflugzeug, das ganz in der Nähe gebaut worden war und eine Entfernung von insgesamt 120 Fuß zurücklegte und dabei 12 Sekunden in der Luft blieb.

Die Luftfahrt hat seit jenem ersten Flug Riesenfortschritte gemacht. Im Museum, das in der Nähe des Nationaldenkmals der Gebrüder Wright liegt, können die Besucher diesen ersten Flug im Nachbau des berühmten Flugzeuges nachempfinden.

印象的なケープ・ハッテラス・ナショナル海岸（右）同岬の灯台は一般に公開されている。このレンガ造りの193フィートの灯台は1870年に建設され〝アトランティックの墓地〟のパノラマを望む。ハッテラスは東部海岸の漁業の村として有名で、オクラコック島へ行くには立寄らねばならない場所である。

キル・デビル・ヒルの上に厳かに立つ60´の記念碑は、1903年12月17日のライト兄弟による初めてのグライダーによる飛行を記念している。付近の建物で組立てられた最初の飛行機は、12秒空中に止まり120フィートを飛行した。飛行技術はこの最初の飛行の成功から目覚ましい発展を遂げた。ライト兄弟国立記念碑近くに立つ博物館で、来訪者はこの最初の飛行機の復刻版に当時のドラマチックな飛行を彷彿とすることができる。

Dominante Cape Hatteras National Scashore (derecha), el Faro de Cape Hatteras está abierto al público. Esta torre de ladrillos, alta 193 pies construida en 1870, se extiende sobre el "Cementerio del Atlántico". Hatteras es una de las localidades de pesca más famosas de la Costa Oriental y parada obligatoria para la Isla de Ocracocke.

Construido majestuosamente sobre la Kill Devil Hill, el monumento de 60' celebra el vuelo de los Hermanos Wright sobre el primer aeroplano de motor, el 17 de Diciembre de 1903. Después de ser construido en los edificios cercanos, el primer avión voló durante 12 segundos y realizó una distancia total de 120 pies.

La aviación ha hecho grandes pasos adelante desde el primer vuelo. En el museo que está cerca del Monumento Nacional de los Hermanos Wright, los visitantes pueden revivir aquel primer vuelo en la reproducción del avión de los Hermanos Wright.

Wright Brothers Memorial ▶
ライト兄弟メモリアル

Currituck Beach Lighthouse. Phare de Currituck Beach. Leuchtturm von Currituck Beach. キャリタック・ビーチ灯台 *Faro de Currituck Beach*

Currituck Beach Lighthouse at Corolla is just south of Virginia. It is solid red brick and has been guiding mariners to safety since December, 1875.

Le Currituck Beach Lighthouse à Corolla se trouve au sud de la Virginie. Depuis décembre 1875, cette solide tour en briques a sauvé de nombreux marins.

Das Currituck Beach Lighthouse in Corolla liegt südlich von Virginia. Der solide rote Ziegelsteinbau geleitet die Seeleute seit Dezember 1875 sicher in den Hafen.

コロッラのキャリタック・ビーチの灯台はバージニアの南に位置する。この赤いレンガの堅牢な灯台は1875年から海の男達を安全へと導いて来た。

El Currituck Beach Lighthouse en Corolla se encuentra en el sur de Virginia. Sólida torre de ladrillos rojos que ha llevado a salvo a los marineros desde Diciembre de 1875.

Cape Hatteras. Cap Hatteras. Cape Hatteras. ハッテラス岬 *Cabo Hatteras*

Ocracoke Lighthouse is the oldest lighthouse operating on the North Carolina coast. It has been in operation since 1823.

Ocracoke Lighthouse est le plus vieux phare de la côte de la Caroline du Nord. Il fonctionne depuis 1823.

Ocracoke Lighthouse ist der älteste Leuchtturm der Küste von North Carolina. Er funktioniert seit 1823.

オクラコク灯台はノースカロライナ州海岸で最古の灯台である。1823年から稼働。

Ocracoke Lighthouse es el faro más viejo de la costa de Carolina del Norte. Está activo desde 1823.

Ocracoke Lighthouse & Harbor. Phare et port d'Ocracoke. Leuchtturm und Hafen von Ocracoke. オクラコクの灯台と港 *Faro y puerto de Ocracoke*

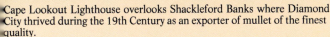

Cape Lookout Lighthouse overlooks Shackleford Banks where Diamond City thrived during the 19th Century as an exporter of mullet of the finest quality.

Cape Lookout Lighthouse domine Shackleford Banks, où Diamond City prospéra au XIXe siècle en tant qu'exportatrice de rougets de premier choix.

Cape Lookout Lighthouse überragt Shackleford Banks, wo Diamond City im XIX. Jahrhundert durch den Export erstklassiger Meerbarben eine Blütezeit erlebte.

ケープ・ルックアウト灯台が、19世紀に最上品質のボラの輸出地として繁栄したダイヤモンド・シティーのある、シェクルフォードの岸壁を見下ろす。

Bodie Island Lighthouse domina Shackleford Banks, donde Diamond City prosperó en el siglo XIX como exportador de salmonetes de primera cualidad.

Bodie Island Lighthouse was built in 1872 and marks the dangerous stretch of low-lying coast between Capes Henry and Hatteras.

Construit en 1872, Bodie Island Lighthouse éclaire le fragment de côte dangereux entre les Caps Henry et Hatteras.

Bodie Island Lighthouse wurde 1872 erbaut und beleuchtet die gefährliche Küstenstrecke zwischen Cape Henry und Cape Hatteras.

ボダイ島の灯台は1872年に建設され、ケープス・ヘンリーとハッテラス間の危険な区域を照らしている。

Bodie Island Lighthouse ha sido construido en 1872 e ilumina el peligroso trecho de costa entre Capes Henry y Hatteras.

Lighthouses of the Outer Banks

The sea has always played a major role in shaping the history of the North Carolina Outer Banks and it still does today. A warm offshore current, the Gulf Stream, flows north and veers eastward north of Cape Hatteras. Spanish treasure fleets returning from the mines of Mexico and Central America made good use of this north-bound current in their voyages to Spain. Southbound vessels followed an inshore counter-current of colder water, a branch of the Labrador Current. These might have been two very efficient marine super-highways, except that at Cape Hatteras, the Gulf Stream pinches down on the inshore Labrador Current and forces southbound ships into a narrow passage around Diamond Shoals, the partially submerged fingers of shifting sand that jut more than 10 miles out from the Cape. More than 500 ships of many nations, trying to find their way around the shoals have foundered at or near Cape Hatteras, earning the area the reputation as the "Graveyard of the Atlantic." There are many shipwrecks either visible in the water or washed ashore within the Cape Hatteras Seashore. Lighthouses were erected to prevent further tragedies along the coastal shoals.

L'océan a toujours joué et joue encore un rôle déterminant dans l'histoire des Outer Banks de la Caroline du Nord. Le courant chaud du Golfe coule au nord et vire à l'est au nord du Cap Hatteras. Les flottes espagnoles, de retour des mines du Mexique et d'Amérique Centrale avec leurs précieux chargements, surent exploiter ces courants lors de leurs voyages vers l'Espagne. Les vaisseaux allant vers le sud suivaient un courant contraire d'eau plus froide, faisant partie du courant du Labrador, en direction de la côte. Ces deux courants auraient pu être de véritables "autoroutes" marines si ce n'est qu'à hauteur du Cap Hatteras, le courant du Golfe se heurte au courant du Labrador qui se dirige vers le sud et pousse les bateaux dans cette direction, à travers un passage étroit entre les bas-fonds de Diamond, des langues de sables mouvants partiellement submergées par l'eau qui s'étendent sur plus de 10 miles. Alors qu'ils tentaient de trouver un passage entre ces bas-fonds, plus de 500 bateaux de nationalité différentes ont coulé autour du Cap Hatteras, ce qui a valu a ce site le surnom de "Cimetière de l'Atltantique". Du littoral du Cap Hatteras, on peut voir de nombreuses épaves qui affleurent ou qui sont poussées vers la rive. Les phares ont été construits pour que cessent ce genre de tragédies.

Das Meer hat in der Geschichte der Outer Banks von North Carolina immer eine bedeutende Rolle gespielt und ist auch heute noch wichtig. Der warme Golfstrom fließt im Norden und wendet sich nördlich von Cape Hatteras nach Osten. Die spanischen Flotten, die mit ihrer kostbaren Ladung aus den Bergwerken Mexikos und Zentralamerikas kamen, nutzten diese warme, nördlich gerichtete Strömung bei ihren Reisen nach Spanien. Die dem Süden zusteuernden Schiffe folgten der entgegengesetzten, kälteren Strömung in Richtung Küste, einem Nebenfluß des Labrador Stroms. Zwei ideale "Schnellstraßen" des Meers, sollte man annehmen, würde der Golfstrom nicht bei Cape Hatteras auf den in Küstenrichtung fließenden Labradrostrom treffen und die Schiffe nach Süden treiben, in eine enge Durchfahrt um die Untiefen von Diamond, teilweise überflutete Fließsand-Landzungen, die sich über 10 km vom Kap erstrecken. Über 500 Schiffe aus aller Herren Länder sind beim Versuch, die Untiefen zu umschiffen, vor Cape Hatteras versunken, was dem Gebiet den Namen "Friedhof des Atklantiks" eintrug. Von der Küste von Cape Hatteras aus kann man zahlreiche Wracks erkennen, die aus dem Wasser auftauchen oder in Richtung des Ufers getrieben werden. Die Leuchttürme wurden gebaut, um künftig Tragödien an den Untiefen der Küste zu vermeiden.

Currituck Beach Lighthouse - 1875
Phare de Currituck Beach - 1875
Leuchtturm von Currituck Beach - 1875
キュリタック・ビーチ灯台 -1875
Faro de Currituck Beach - 1875

Bodie Island Lighthouse - 1872
Phare de l'Ile Bodie - 1872
Leuchtturm der Insel Bodie - 1872
ボダイ島灯台 -1872
Faro de la Isla Bodie - 1872

ノースカロライナ州の外海の砂州の歴史の形成には、海が常に決定的な役割を果たして来たし現在でも果たしている。湾の暖流が北に流れハッテラス岬の北で東に方向転換する。メキシコや中央アメリカの鉱山から貴金属の荷を積んで引返すスペイン船隊が、スペインに戻る船旅にこの北に向かう潮流を利用した。南に向かう戦闘用帆船は反対に海岸地帯に向かう寒流、ラブラドル海流の支流に乗った。まるで素晴らしい2つの海の高速道路である。しかし、湾の潮流が海岸に向かうラブラドル海流に出会うハッテラス岬付近には、部分的に波に流動する砂で覆われ岬から10マイル以上にも渡り広がっているダイヤモンドの砂州があり、その周囲の狭い海路の中を、船を南に押流す。様々な国の500以上の船が砂州区域を越える海路を見つけようとして、ハッテラス岬付近で難破しており、このことからこの海域は"大西洋の墓場"と呼ばれている。ハッテラス岬の海岸からは海面から顔を出したり、岸に押上げられたりしている多くの難破船の残骸を見る事ができる。いくつかの灯台がこれ以上の悲劇を繰り返さないために海岸付近の砂州地帯に設置された。

El mar ha jugado siempre un papel determinante al plasmar la historia de las Outer Banks de Carolina del Norte y lo tiene incluso hoy. La calida corriente del Golfo fluye hacia el norte y gira hacia oriente, al norte de Cabo Hatteras. Las flotas españolas, de vuelta de las minas de Mexico y de América Central con su preciosa carga, hicieron buen uso de esta corriente directa al norte, en sus viajes hacia España. Los navíos directos al sur seguían una corriente contraria de agua más fría, directa hacia la costa, una rama de la corriente del Labrador. Podrían haber sido dos "autovías" marinas muy eficaces, si no fuese porque en el Cabo Hatteras, la corriente del Golfo se encuentra con la corriente del Labrador directa hacia la costa y empuja las naves hacia el sur, en un estrecho paso en torno a los bancos de Diamond, lenguas parcialmente sumergidas de arenas movedizas que se extienden a lo largo de más de 10 millas del Cabo. Más de 500 naves de diferentes nacionalidades, en el intento de encontrar un paso para superar los bancos de arena, han naufragado en torno al Cabo Hatteras, dando a la zona la reputación de "Cementerio del Atlántico". Desde el litoral de Cabo Hatteras se pueden ver muchos restos de naves, que sobresalen del agua o que son empujadas a la orilla. Los faros han sido construidos para evitar futuras tragedias a lo largo de los bancos costeros.

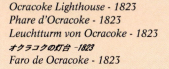

Cape Hatteras Lighthouse - 1870
Phare du Cap Hatteras - 1870
Leuchtturm von Cape Hatteras - 1870
ハッテラス岬の灯台 -1870
Faro de Cabo Hatteras - 1870

Ocracoke Lighthouse - 1823
Phare d'Ocracoke - 1823
Leuchtturm von Ocracoke - 1823
オクラコクの灯台 -1823
Faro de Ocracoke - 1823

Cape Lookout Lighthouse - 1859
Phare du Cap Lookout - 1859
Leuchtturm von Cape Lookout - 1859
ルックアウト岬の灯台 -1859
Faro de Cabo Lookout - 1859

Outer Banks

Wind Surfing along the Outer Banks is a fast growing sport. Watching the shrimp boats come in all along the coast is another treat, but eating the fresh shrimp is the best treat of all.

De plus en plus de monde vient surfer le long des Outer Banks. Certains prendront également plaisir à voir rentrer les bateaux de pêche, et encore plus à déguster de délicieuses crevettes.

Surfen ist an den Outer Banks ein Sport, der immer beliebter wird. Die Fischerboote in den Hafen einlaufen zu sehen ist ein weiteres Vergnügen, aber ein noch größerer Genuß ist es, anschließend die Garnelen zu verspeisen.

アウターバンクスでのサーフィンは、近年益々盛んになっている。漁船が戻ってくるのを見るのはまた別の楽しみであるが、それよりもさらに楽しみなのは海老の味である。

La práctica del surf a lo largo de las Outer Banks es una actividad cada vez más común. Ver regresar las barcas de pesca es otro placer, pero un placer aún más grande es el de comer las gambas.

From commercial fishing to the sport fisherman, fishing is a favorite pastime on the North Carolina Outer Banks.

De la pêche commerciale à l'activité sportive, la pêche est un des passe-temps favoris sur les Outer Banks de la Caroline du Nord.

Von der Gewerblichen Fischerei zum Sportangeln ist das Fischen an den Outer Banks von North Carolina einer der beliebtesten Zeitverbreibe.

商業向けの漁からスポーツの釣りまでノースカロライナ州のアウターバンクスで最も好まれる娯楽の一つは釣りである。

Desde la pesca comercial hasta la actividad practicada como deporte, la pesca es uno de los pasatiempos preferidos en las Outer Banks de Carolina del Norte.

Ferries are an important part of the transportation system along the Outer Banks. The transfer of people and vehicles between island and the mainland is provided by ferries.

Les ferrys jouent un rôle important dans le dispositif de transport le long des Outer Banks, en transportant les personnes et les véhicules entre l'île et le continent.

Die Fährschiffe spielen für das Verkehrssystem der Outer Banks eine bedeutende Rolle. Die Personen- und Fahrzeugbeförderung zwischen der Insel und dem Festland wird durch Fährschiffe garantiert.

アウターバンクス沿いの輸送システムでは、連絡船が重要な役割を果たす。陸地と島の間の人と車の輸送は連絡船により賄われている。

Las lanchas desarrollan un papel importante en el sistema de transportes a lo largo de las Outer Banks. El transporte de personas y vehículos entre la isla y la tierra firme está garantizado por las lanchas.

Outer Banks

Walking along the Outer Banks is a pleasure no matter what type of weather, as the beauty must be seen to be believed. Manteo is a lovely coastal town, and home of the Elizabeth II.

Se promener le long des Outer Banks est très agréable, quelles que soient les conditions météo, car leur beauté est incroyable. Manteo est une gracieuse petite ville côtière où vécut Elisabeth II.

Es ist bei jedem Wetter ein Vergnügen, an den Outer Banks spazierenzugehen, weil man ihren landschaftlichen Reiz gesehen haben muß, um ihn zu verstehen. Manteo ist ein hübsches Küstenstädtchen und Wohnsitz von Elizabeth II.

アウターバンクス沿いの散歩はどんな天候でも楽しい。美しさを理解するには見る他はない。マンテオは海浜の可愛い町でエリザベス2世の居住地でもあった。

Pasear a lo largo de las Outer Banks es un placer, cualquiera que sean las condiciones atmosféricas, porque es necesario ver la belleza para creer. Manteo es una graciosa localidad costera y demora de Isabel II.

▼

Ocracoke is famous for its beautiful wild ponies believed to be descendants of shipwrecked Spanish mustangs.

Ocracoke est célèbre pour ses splendides poneys sauvages qui, d'après certains, sont les descendants des mustangs espagnols rescapés d'un naufrage.

Ocracoke ist berühmt für seine prächtigen wilden Ponys, die von den spanischen Mustangs, die infolge eines Schiffsbruchs an Land gelangten, abstammen sollen.

オクラコクは素晴らしい野生の小馬ポニーで有名であり、難破で漂着したスペイン種野生馬ムスタングの末裔であると言われている。

Ocracoke es famosa por sus esplendidos ponies salvajes, que se dice descendían de los mustang españoles llegados a tierra durante un naufragio.

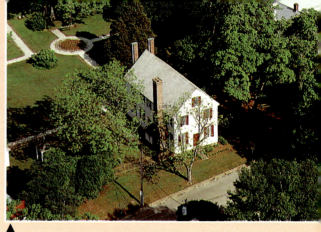

▲
Historic Bath House
Etablissement balnéaire historique
Historische Badeanstalt
歴史ある海水浴場の家
Establecimiento balneario histórico

▼ *Manteo*
マンテオ

◀ Cape Hatteras
Cap Hatteras
Cape Hatteras
ハッテラス岬
Cabo Hatteras

▼ Silver Lake Harbor Dock
Quai portuaire du lac Silver
Hafenmole des Silver Sees
シルバー湖の港の波止場
Muelle del puerto del Lago Silver

▲
"Carolina Moon Keep Shining" over the Outer Banks
"La lune de la Caroline continue de briller" sur les Outer Banks
"Der Mond von Carolina scheint" auf die Outer Banks
アウターバンクスの上に "カロライナの月が輝き続ける"
"La luna de Carolina sigue resplandeciendo" sobre las Outer Banks

▼
Nags Head
ネッグス・ヘッド

Coastal

Oak Island Lighthouse is the southernmost lighthouse along the North Carolina coast.

Le phare de l'île d'Oak est situé à l'extrême sud de la côte de la Caroline du Nord.

Der Leuchtturm der Insel Oak ist der südlichste der Küste von North Carolina.

オーク島の灯台はノースカロライナ州の海域の最南端にある。

El faro de la isla de Oak es el más meridional a lo largo de la costa de Carolina del Norte.

◄

Sea Oats serve a very important purpose along the shores of North Carolina. Acting as a retaining wall, the sea oats grow along the beaches and help to maintain the coastline.

Les sea oats jouent un rôle fondamental le long des côtes de la Caroline du Nord. En poussant le long des plages, elles font office de barrière et protègent le littoral.

Der Sea Oat spielt an den Küsten North Carolinas eine wichtige Rolle, weil er als Barriere dient. Der Sea Oat wächst am Ufer und trägt dazu bei, daß der Strand nicht vom Wasser weggespült wird.

海辺のエンバクはノースカロライナの海岸線で無くてはならない役割を果している。砂浜に生育するこのエンバクはバリケードの役割をし海岸線を保つために一役買っている。

Las sea oats tienen un objeto muy importante a lo largo de las costas de Carolina del Norte. Funcionando como barrera, las sea oats crecen a lo largo de las playas y contribuyen a conservar el litoral.

◄

For many years, Bald Head Island stood alone as the only structure on Smith Island guiding marine craft up the Cape Fear River and past the "feared" naked bleak elbow of sand that juts far into the ocean from lower Cape Fear. This beautiful island can only be accessed by ferry and the primary motorized mode of transportation on the island is golf carts.

Pendant de nombreuses années, la Bald Head Island a été le seul point de repère sur Smith Island, et a guidé les équipages le long du fleuve Cape Fear et au-delà du coude de sable aride et dépouillé qui s'étend sur plusieurs miles dans l'océan à partir de l'extrême pointe inférieure de Cape Fear. Le ferry est le seul moyen d'arriver sur cette île splendide, où l'un des principaux moyens de transport sont des petits fourgons de golf.

Viele Jahre lang war Bald Head Island der einzige Anhaltspunkt auf Smith Island, der die Schiffsbesatzungen entlang dem Fluß Cape Fear und über die gefürchtete Krümmung aus nacktem, ödem Sand hinaus geleitete, die sich von der niedrigsten Spitze von Cape Fear aus etliche Meilen ins Meer erstreckt. Diese herrliche Insel kann nur mit dem Fährschiff erreicht werden, und das wichtigste Transportmittel der Insel besteht aus Golfkarren.

長い年月の間ボールド・ヘッド・アイランドはスミス島で唯一の基点地であった。ケープ・フィアー川を下る船乗りを、河口から海に向い何マイルも広がる危険な裸の砂州の向こう側まで水先案内する役割を果した。この美しい島には連絡船でのみ行きつくことができる。島唯一の交通機関は、ゴルフ用のライトバンである。

Durante muchos años, la Bald Head Island ha sido el único punto de referencia sobre la Smith Island, guiando las tripulaciones a lo largo del rio Cape Fear y más alla de la temida ensenada de arena desnuda y rocosa que se alarga durante muchas millas en el océano, desde la punta inferior de Cape Fear. Esta esplendida isla puede ser alcanzada sólo con la lancha y el principal medio de transporte sobre la isla está constituido por los coches de golf.